HEAVY THINGS

HEAVY THINGS

by

J. G. FINCH

T.N.
Publishing

Printed in the United States of America

First Printing, 2016

ISBN-13: 9780692727638

ISBN-10: 0692727639

TABLE OF CONTENTS

HEAVY THINGS

BANDAGE

I would smoke cigars near my open window alone
because I thought I was secretly boycotting nature itself.

The limitations of life secretly angered me,
so I wrote poem after poem

and the fire in my heart kindled and ruptured as I typed.

      I typed the words:
Silent and complacent I will never live

Smoke flowing out of my lungs—

Coughing until it hurts
Satisfied with the pain in my body
Soon I will be free

Hearing the birds singing outside my window,
as they fight each other for each seed.

PEARLS OF TEARS

Tears are my only freedom.
They are like cheap pearls,
rolling out of the limitations
nature has created.

My mind seeks Heaven,
and it does not understand,

to be born without nature's caressing hands with every breath,
and with every ache,
without a whisper more beautiful and stronger than the fluttering of but-
terfly wings.
Nature should have been an everlasting embrace;
if not, it should have at least created us without a mind to crave a woman's
hands.

A woman's hands are not cheap;
a man works his whole life for them,
and still dies alone within his cold bedroom.

RULES FOR BIRDS

All birds have their own rules and clubs.
And there are many rules to follow:

Rules for chirping
Rules for dancing and bopping
Rules for expressing oneself when singing

And many birds scoff at those that do not follow the other rules given to them by the bird kingdom.

And they hate even worse a crow with a soft crackle or
an owl that loves the daytime and ignores the mice, that would rather eat leaves.

The crows saw the hawk and hated that he was relaxed against a twig of leaves. So they crackled and bopped, and crackled and bopped. But the hawk remained relaxed, ignoring them all.

They were used to hawks coming after their eggs, and as usual, the crows would have fun chasing them in the sky. And because he was a big, power-ful hawk, something had to be wrong with him for not having the desire to steal their eggs, so the crows can fly after him.

Even the house sparrows saw what was going on, and they began to chirp frantically, pointing their small pointy beaks at the hawk from a nearby feeder—except for one sparrow, who always thought differently than the rest.

That sparrow would ignore the rules of the other sparrows around him because he thought they lived life too simple. He always thought living life feeder to feeder was so boring. He loved the way the finches sang and the way the crows planned their attacks in the sky, and he definitely admired a hawk that was free from the rules of other hawks. *Wow, a hawk that stood up against other hawks for his own freedom and uniqueness,* he thought. The other sparrows saw that he admired the hawk so much, they began to scoff at him by violently fluttering their wings and angrily chirping. The hawk quietly watched them all, and finally the sparrows flew away, leaving the young sparrow alone. The sparrow stood on the ground below the feeder by himself looking up at the hawk. The hawk stood silently on a tree branch above; the vulnerable sparrow noticed him watching and happily welcomed him. With a great surprise, the hawk flew down, and the small sparrow bopped in happiness, celebrating their uniqueness. The hawk lowered his head down to the sparrow and grabbed the sparrow, and as a painful and piercing shriek came from the young sparrow's beak, the hawk flew away with an easy meal.

CULT-URE

The black race, the white race, and all races
looked at each other to find approved actions by their members.

It was not logic they went by,
but it was by fear; they watched each other like overseers
one careful step at a time.

GOD IS LOW AND HIGH

I walked upon a sycamore tree and noticed there was more to life than worrying.
I saw new, bright green leaves swaying from its twigs. *Ah, the wind, subtle and delightful,* I thought. And in my mind there was an infinite field of dandelions surrounding me. And what crawled up on my arm were red ants that I observed like a child, marching and singing.

It was God within tiny moving things with many legs mysteriously crawling on my skin.
It was God within the dandelions that drooped low and high.

And I noticed I was happy for once.
I got it. I had insight. It was God that was dying and living.

Then there was a dreadful feeling; I thought about going back to work the next day, and I realized death would be beautiful just as the dying dandelions near my feet.

NUMB TIMES

Ache to ache, I can get by.

Clock into my job today. Smile a little more.

I can get by.

Before I go to sleep—

Crack the bottle open, smell what I will taste.

The dullness of my life come alive.

Baby, maybe, I can get by.

GRAY EYES

At first you go through it,
attempting to do the right thing until you are broken.
Then you learn who smiles lies,
and who lies tries to survive.
Then you learn the nature of life:
There is neither only dark or light.
You are wronged one day,
then the next day you wrong someone else.
You look in the mirror and try not to take yourself so important.
And when they come to strike pain upon you,
you may strike back, but you will be relieved to know you are never innocent.

Then you will learn to look at life with gray eyes.

BABIES

You do not understand a man such as myself?
To be so quiet, but so powerful, even the loudmouths who come running at me will never see the strength and speed of my fist before it is too late.
But that is the only language they understand. I am talking to you, who only speaks rashly and loudly.

And I naturally speak softly but civilized, but you would not understand one word of it.
But for me to fight you, you will have no choice to see my strength. And that will convince you, but then it will scare you away.
Why do all people of all cultures demand power, but when real power is shown, it is feared?

And I am the most peaceful person that will come, but learn to respect it, if not, I am afraid that humanity will keep going on this vicious cycle of stupidity.
There are differences between gangsters and thugs.
Gangsters play a chess game with an aim to gain more money.
Thugs will ball their fist and swing without one plan. Without one thought.

And this is who you respect more than me?

Women want a gangster until they meet the real gangster.

LOOK INTO MY EYES

Look into my eyes

They are not that simple.
I come from a womb of hellfire,
born into a bed of red roses.
How beautiful I look from outside,

and the world never realizes who I am, where I am from.

Look into my eyes

Like the sword of the king who killed many on the battlefield,
but you have forgotten the blood on the blade because the blood washes
off gracefully, as if this sword was never used.

Look into my eyes

From ancient lands where rivers flow,
where no fragile man stands high.

Look into my eyes

A perpetual strength hidden within layers of darkness
far away, in an infinite reservoir of depth, waiting, lonely but never broken.

If they were exposed to my world, they would see the crumbling of their
small, beating hearts, from each potential intimate touch of my hands that
is always overlooked, that is always misunderstood.

Look into my eyes

My body blistered and rough but slowly healed by my own isolation, hidden in some cave over long periods of time. And if you chose to touch me, you would feel the coldness of mountaintops, and the beauty of an endless field of potential

frozen . . .

But my smile is warm as the embrace of a deceased love. Although I am truly sincere, I cannot smile as brightly as I did so many years ago.

Can't you see that I have been through the depths of hell,
and I'm slowly but surely coming full circle to walk and appreciate the emptiness of the wind, and the bareness of my feet emerged softly in this morning soil?
Can you understand, my smile isn't weak? I only now seek to escape the deep wounds I kept hidden from my past. I am now giving life another try. I am walking out of this darkness into the warmth of the sun.

Finally can you see my eyes?

WHY THE ARTIST

When the heart brews slowly and his passion welds his soul with its flame and hammer, unwillingly and screaming, he has no choice but to become an artist.

He must write, he must sculpt, he must paint. He must do these things to defeat the limitations nature created, not because he wants to, but because he has no choice.

Although nature can be beautiful, he can never find among it an embrace his heart desires.

And there he is, under some tree, writing it out about hands made of some type of mist, gently touching his forehead in the shade of a tree, when the first cool winds of winter begin.

If this could only happen every night, it would make the view of the mountains more beautiful, as well as the dark hollows, the trees, the birds' songs in the morning.

Then love would last until his last breath, instead of the emptiness and the absence of an ongoing touch.

To live life without it—to have only the eyes tiredly gazing at the distant stars above and the empty, dull blaze of the sun, night after day, until death—would mean to live but would mean to live in hell!

NOELANI AWAITS

I

You waited there, alluring what was never spoken.
Hips shapely, soft, and bare, hidden from the sun.
Your feet in the cool, sparkling water between stones,
among large clusters of trees.

I saw you waiting for me without words.
I saw you examining my wounds from over the years from a distance, with
your back turned and your face to the side.
I knew you were waiting for me.

The smell of pine wood faintly in the air.
The rustling of leaves on long, tall, haunting trees, surrounding us like
gates from the world.
The sound of water between,
gently moving from one hidden place to another.

The darkness, my hunger—
I want to cry deep, forgive me.
I know you're waiting for me.

II

Tears fell from his eyes like blood from a punctured heart over large, dry
stones.
He slumped down to the ground, weeping deeply.
And the winds increased.

The stones under him, wet-dripping-warm.
And from then on, the sun never flickered upon his skin again.
His aching hands laid lifeless.
And the world turned, unknowingly.

III

What he had desired before the blade was in his hand
was her hands softly warm on his arms,
and to close his eyes for years and wake up to see her near.

Even her wounded dark brown arms tightly pressed around his body, or
her rosy, lonely cheeks softly touching his face among tears, forehead to
forehead, without cheap words or lips touching would have been satisfying.

He even admired the imperfections of her face: moles and blemishes,
because, in his mind, they were all carefully flowered by God's imperfect
strokes.
And the lines on her aged face that stretched out from the corners of her
eyes, because when he saw them, he saw a subtle, calm wisdom the world
blindly could not see.

IV

He was a painter, who worked a few menial jobs on the side, singing as he
worked.
Happy as the sun. Gentle as the walk of a giraffe. His build lissome, his
stride delicate and graceful. But being somewhat soft spoken and extremely
earnest, it was difficult for him to become more businesslike like the other
powerful men.
Not one inch of him could charge as powerful as a lion, or beat his chest
like those manly men in suits, with their heads high, speaking assertive
demands. Those were men like his father and brother whom he admired,
but he knew deep down he was different.

V

As a young boy, his family knew he was unlike the other children around him. One day, his father caught him staring at the new shoots of wildflowers growing in the front lawn and gazing at the sun in the morning, then quietly running back into the house to sit still in silence. His family was wide-eyed to see such a young boy do these types of things as grown-ups do. Then, his father finally questioned him. "Why are you so deep, my boy? Why don't you do what other young boys do?" He did not reply. Offended and shocked at what his father had said, he tried his best to mask his likings as much as he could. But over time, he discovered he had a great interest and talent in painting, so he decided to focus on painting more than anything. When he became an adult, he became a painter who was recognized as brilliant to some of the locals, but the problem was that his paintings were too abstract for the likings of many people, especially those who were considered important in the art world.

VI

His lovers would come to visit him in his small apartment, and he was always working on several paintings at once. And there were things he said to them that most did not understand.
"Come here, sit down, and I will paint, and you will do as you please."
He did not mention sex, but he did mention the essence of her.
"I won't tell you about these beautiful things we have all the time.
They are things that cannot be described in words. And I am here, with you, and you are with me." As he smiled with a quiet confidence, as he continued to put strokes of paint on the canvas.
"I will be the consistent love in your life, loving you no matter what. That is what the world doesn't have. Although I can't buy you the greatest things in life at the moment, you're my only commitment, and there are my jobs that will get us through, and my paintings, and there will be new beginnings and new adventures that will come in our lives."

They stayed for months but all of them eventually left, lacking patience with great misunderstanding, but sincerely wishing him the best that life could bring him. They needed something more practical, like more money to buy the things they wanted, and a home, not a small one-bedroom apartment full of paintings.

He would painfully understand their reasons, sometimes tearing up alone, wondering whether he give up on what he loves the most to be married, because he was so attached to the idea of love, it drove him almost mad. But sometimes he did attempt to become the man they wanted, but it felt like he was walking in shoes that were not his own. He actually felt like he was wearing small, tight, stuffy shoes. It would hurt to the point he wanted to sit down, and pull them off with relief. Every inch of his flesh, and every inch of his soul throbbed painfully. Year after year he painted without getting the recognition he wanted, and things slowly went downhill. With only his small admirers at his art galleries and shows, he barely survived as a painter. He eventually became older, and to a great degree, he withdrew himself from the public, continuing to paint in his cluttered one-bedroom apartment.

VII

One day he daydreamed about some beautiful escape as he stared at the clouds in the sky. At that moment of thought, large, dark clouds parted from the long bright rays of the sun. His eyes gazed intensely on a billowing mist, dissolving amongst large mountains covered in clusters of tall green trees. In his tired mind, this was the most beautiful thing he had ever seen. It fact, it somehow reminded him of the beauty he longed for within a woman. He thought about how he could beautifully escape, and pensively a smile slowly began to surface on his rugged face, and the name Noelani came out of his lips, meaning the mist of heaven.

And each year, his desire to meet her increased. And to him, she was elusive as the winds, appearing as mist, moving among streams of water, quietly stalking between trees. She was here to love those who had too much love to give, who could not find the same love in return. Each year, he put a few strokes on the canvas, painting her slowly and carefully. Then he would examine his emotions and the strokes he painted. He would sometimes question his plans for meeting her, but sadly he wanted to follow through. In his mind, she stood in the forest, beautiful and naked, waiting for his embrace. This was the only way he could comfortably find his way out of his deep longing he had his whole life. He did not feel sorry for himself, despite his handicap to never rise as other men had risen through business or by moving up in one of his menial odd jobs.

VIII

It was hell, to feel so strongly about love but never have the opportunity to feel the same intensity of a beating heart near, and to never feel a hand that embraced his hand, never lasting more than a year.

In his eyes, his life was vain, and life had no purpose.
Life was camouflaged as God's beautiful design on the surface,
but upon a closer observation, it began to cheapen and become tasteless.

And although the ocean appeared infinite and powerful,
although flowers showed off their intriguing colors to his senses, boasting together on the open fields under the sun, it was all nothing if there was not one fleshly woman consistent in his life to embrace the same beauty nature emulated.

A WEALTHY LADY

If you didn't know, magnolia flowers blossom in June.
It represents the beginning of summer.
An elderly dark-skinned woman with smooth plum skin and a large decorative hat picks one carefully and places it in a bowl of water in the center of the table of her living room.
She walks inside her bedroom and closes the door.
In the living room, a summer breeze follows through the screen of the window.
And there, an elegant warm touch of fragrance in the air like an extension of her spirit.
There is always this majestic presence when speaking her name.

Mrs. Taylor
Mrs. Brown . . .

Somehow immortal she feels when you are in her presence.
What is her magic? How does she do that thing? That thing only a wise man can understand.

A PRETTY WOMAN

There is more to a pretty woman than a pretty face.

There she is, looking at us with a frown because of something we did, and we embarrassingly don't want to see that she is not easily amused, because we passively want everything to go our way.

As if we want her to smile at us on command.
Just as we want her to acknowledge us just because we exist.

We would hide her knowing eyes against us if we could,
and then we would hide our mistakes and expect the world from a pretty face.

We forget women also go to the restroom.
They also sweat, blow their noses, and become sick.

We forget they also feel pain, and have the ability to rightfully choose because they, too, have a brain.

Our feelings are hurt when a beautiful woman does not adhere to our desires.

I, too, for many years felt the same, and now I have learned.

The truth places a mirror to my ugly face and my piggish desires.
The truth pulls me out of the warm, isolated womb of my mind into the openness of truth.

Men, we are not as innocent as we believe.
Women, we are learning you are not just some doll for our pleasures.

However, men and women are born with different cards playing at the same table.

Going home with the same victories.
Going to bed with the same failures.

I STAND TALL

I want to be deeper than God
and warmer than the sun.

And those who hear these words,
who quote word for word from what they've been taught,
come in single file

stomping their spears
and cocking their guns.

I smile because I know my heart is more valuable than the limitations of
life itself.

It is more valuable than anything that grows and then withers.

It's more valuable than the lies of oneness in marriage
and the temporary touch of a lover's hand.

My heart will not stop its protest until my last breaths are with her, hand in
hand, and then until death, heart to heart.

That is my heart's only way to see immortality.

But I know that without action, the passion of the heart destroys the body,
just like a tree with damaged roots that no longer bears fruit.

That is why I stand tall when I am outnumbered among those who are too
dense to truly understand that real love requires a grueling effort,

and that is when I proudly look down at my beating heart and the muscles
in my arms: *the most beautiful and tangible tools a man can own.*

PAINTING IN THE DARK

Just because I love you don't mean I'm going to let you know.
Just know that I think about you every day.
And if I'm not dealing with you, I'm probably not dealing with no one.
My life is edgy, beautiful and intense.
Kind of like walking a thin rope in the sky
while painting a picture of a beautiful place I can call home.

I CHOOSE TO IGNORE

Didn't care if I died,
but at the same time I meditated
with alcohol along with ladies
from the streets.
At night they wondered about me,
like I thought about them.
I thought the way they moved was like poetry.
I was born a lover and loner
who thought of all movements of life as different art forms.
I would wander in the most dangerous neighborhoods
because I was in love with death and life.
Since I was a kid, I had dreams about how I was supposed to move the
world, but really I just want to move in my heart.

But one day I won't be selfish.
One day I will let the world know who I am.
One day I will not be afraid.
But until then
I will enjoy these so-called lowly things I call life.

HANGING ON

Sometimes I give up
and feel this toxic self-pity
that is so painful and potent.
Affecting my mind and body.
Sleeping in toxic guilt.
Shadows of my past I want to leave behind.
I get up to dust myself again
because I want to live again.
I look in the mirror and smile again.
I got to feel some pride
to know that I am grateful.
To know that I can't live in the past
although the past still affects my body.
I am aware life goes on.
I am going strong
and if I fall again, it is fine.
I will keep getting up until it is my time to die.

A PROSTITUTE SPEAKS

I love the way my blood rushes when
heavy things,
heart pains bring you.

My playground is the dark street that I love.
It's a precious poison that stimulates me,
brings this numb face into light.

My eyes spark
when you moan,
when the money flickers in my hands.

I got the power,
and I smile at you giving me your power.
How you admire my strength,
how you betray your wife.

The new adventure and
fresh, mysterious air
flowing through the windows of your car
as you drive late nights, searching for me.

The foreshadowing of debt creeps in the shadows, waiting—
The collision screams ahead.

Then you try your best,
going to church, saying short prayers,
looking at your wife with secrets.
Humbly you want to apologize.
Then nights come to pass.

You're intoxicated downstairs in the bathroom
while your wife sleeps.
Your phone shaking in your hand,
whispering to me in the late hours.

Orange Grove and Los Robles

WHEN MEN BECOME OLDER

I

I have always wondered about the women who flirt with me when I'm sitting alone. Some rich, some poor. It is not as important as it used to be. I know deep down, once the mystery is gone, it will end.

I know they are like us men. Though they often do things more astuciously, their desires are the same as ours.

I would be a fool to believe they are saints and angels. It is a funny thing to listen to young men and their attempts to win affection from each beautiful woman who walks by.

Then there is a time in your life when you think you are becoming wiser, like all those other men before you. You try to restrain yourself by having more control, to focus on endeavors that are more heartfelt and all the purities of life.

There is always that woman you have seen so many times before, walking in your direction to some place of work or someplace to meet up with someone else. I want you to take note of what I am trying to say—*a beautiful woman will never go to any destination to be alone.* You hear the clacking of her heels assertively hitting the concrete, and you gaze in her direction, noticing her shape, her legs, her facial expression, but you forcefully turn your head away this time, hoping you have something better than her. And after not giving her the attention you believe she expected, you feel a triumphing emotion that you keep to yourself. You try to distance yourself from these women in your own way, stopping the urge within to pursue their affections, to dive into the other mysteries and beauties of life . . . the shimmering red and yellow leaves swaying in a distant field on scattered myrtle trees, or what awaits singing in the deep blackness amongst the stars . . . Why do we live life amongst this untouched beauty, ignoring it all to chase and worship a woman as if we are so powerless, we have the willpower of a five-year-old?

II

Over time, you find that there is no depth in anything other than your own thoughts. All things have a function, and emotion is not one of them. The world was created to be efficient—efficient in birth and death. What you see is what you get, and you can't share this urge with no one—that underlying hunger for a deeper transcendence of love. You cannot do so with a woman because you can only be together as her actor. You become married, and you live a life not of your own, but at least it is somewhat better than being alone.

III

You grow older, and you still hope to stumble on something profound in life, but you find out it's just a dead end. Then, you think of the possibility of experiencing what we call spirituality privately in your mind, but again, another dead end.

You learn only to live privately in thought with your wife, passing your time halfway smiling through life. Doing the best you can like everyone else, now knowing what you always searched for privately cannot be obtained.

IV

You learn that your heart beats what the religious men seek. You feel the common man's pain. He, too, attends church, privately searching for an everlasting beauty and love that will even outlive the temporally fleshly cold hands of his own wife!

V

We think of such escape in religion, and it is called heaven. But how tangible is it, heaven, a place we cannot see? What a shame to desire another place and hate our mundane state now. Why do we live here, to only want another place? Shouldn't we enjoy life now? Why wait to die to enjoy life?

For us who want more than the pleasures of flesh, why do our hearts beat wiser than our entire physical being, which was made by lust?

VI

But can heaven be between the legs of a woman?

Five minutes, ten minutes, even thirty minutes of pleasure
will cost you more than you can ever afford.

To a woman, after sex, indirectly and passively you will always be in her debt.

No, heaven does not put you in debt.

Heaven is everlasting.
Heaven isn't just the satisfaction of our full stomachs—
It quenches the aches within.

That is something most people cannot understand.
This is why I go on my own way, drinking, writing, and dying a slow death.

COUGAR

The love
for the taste of pain,
like the smell of flesh bathed in
expensive perfume
on a cold-hearted bitch
who feels alone.
Her frown is felt like almost death,
like large, dark clouds without the rain.
I kiss her lips, never attempting to save her, but I'm hooked on her
poison and pain.

I breathe her in slow
as she smiles.
She likes the way I kiss
her neck,
which is felt
like an aura of bitter, potent heaviness,
arousing and malignant, flowing
in my stomach, chest into my brain.

I fall between her legs
as my body tingles to numbness.
I feel kind of brave
as I sacrifice my youth,
wrapped tight, pressed to her breasts.
I reach to go but she comforts me to stay,
to marinate in her poison and pain.

I nearly fall asleep.
I become weak,
aroused,
confused,
don't know what to do as I view her husband's clothes hanging in the closet.

My eyes become blurry.
I stop thinking,
heart starts beating,
wish I used a condom.

Don't know what to do,
feeling afraid,
kind of ashamed.
Mixed feelings overwhelm me.

I now plan for my escape.

AN OLDER WOMAN

I

Subtle her smile

She wins me

Subtly her finesse

She then again wins me

Even if she lies, let it be a captivating lie.

I want that better than the nakedness of women.

Sex is great but cheap.

But what is subtle is richer, not holier than.

II

She finally spoke to me and all things around me narrowed in.

She knew an old way of making my heart feel like it never felt before.

I smiled with amazement. *How did she make me feel that way?*

Where did she learn the old ways?

WITCH'S DEFEAT

She listens to you,
smiles with you,
goes to dinners with you,
talks about music with you,
has you open until
you slip and fall.
She's been waiting on it,
told her friends to get ready for it.
She told them where she is going to bite you hard
because you told her your weaknesses when you were drunk.
How much money you make,
your goals, dreams, and fears.
She would caress your face and tell you it's okay.
It felt so right for you at that time.
You felt free to finally lose your mind,
and now you are on the ground,
blood trickling down your side,
her teeth deep in your neck,
while you try to breathe for air.
The word "stop" tries to release from your lips
but it never escapes.
She gets up to make a phone call
and you can't believe what she says.
Blood on her teeth,
fierceness in her eyes,
confidence you have never seen.
As you try to put your head up, she softly rubs your face with the warmest
smile.
She says, "Sweety . . . It's okay."
She then says, "You're having my baby . . . It's okay . . . "

"I already have my lawyers, and let's take this to court."
As your head hits the ground she makes another phone call again in a husky voice.
She says,

"I got him.
I got him . . . "

She keeps the phone near her face as she rubs your dick.

"I got him.
I got him . . . "

Like it was a joke you didn't comprehend.

A SON WHO PRAYED

I asked my Father above, "Why is life so mediocre? Are there any other things you could have created?"

Then my Father came home very late that night, stumbling drunk, with two cheap bottles of beer in his hand.

He was so drunk, before he made it past me into the hallway, he paused, then cringed.

He was telling me he drank all he could and he couldn't drink anymore.

With deep emotional wounds in my chest and insatiable hands, I reached out to grab his halfway drunken bottle, like some deprived prisoner who craved life deeply.

And what I thought was cheap was then so necessary.

Then my Father was relieved to know I was now enlightened.

MAN IN CAR, TINTED WINDOWS

I really don't believe in romance anymore.
That is sad, coming from a dreamer, but I understand.
Razor blades of pain, tears of emptiness.
Now I got to get the hell out of this hellhole.
Be bold and work a dangerous job to get paid high, to get the lust the rats
will wait in line for. Now it's a cold world,
and I told you Ms. Thing, I was better then than I am now.

FOLLOWING SANDRA IN NEW ORLEANS

Heaviness painfully throbbed your beating heart,
as the world could not understand it
and could never see it.
With your slurred words
and tired, dilated eyes,
I smiled, knowing you were not from here,
watching you drenched in sweat,
dripping down from your neck
in the midst of this muggy

      unforsaken place.

And as the last song of thunderous sounds from trumpets played
while golden horns slowly waved in and out of the dark,
screaming to a high climax then falling low
and lower as if it was a rhythm of a train in the rain,

      slowing making its stop,

many along the walls stood whispering to others
while gazing back and forth in your direction
as those at their tables whispered amongst cigarette smoke,
using their empty glasses as ashtrays.

And miserably, you walked towards me across the room with courage, and I
already knew, just like the others, life had already broken you.

And I waited on the other side with a smile until you arrived,
as you stumbled, drunkenly aroused— into my web.

Then your eyes followed my hips outside the front door.

We walked further away from the departing crowd.

And further away.
Then further away

      into darkness,

             then

you heard the sound of car doors mysteriously opening.
Footsteps crept closer, and you searched and strained your eyes to see what was waiting.
And when you saw them, you were suddenly

           transfixed

You cautiously called my name to get an understanding.
And there was a sound of a closing door,
and I had vanished away.

Desperate scrambling sparked, with a quick touch of a blade to your neck.

Movements pushed and pulled against each other
and a sound of fumbling,
finally ending with a loud screech—

        silence.

Heavy footsteps quickly ran away, and time had stood still.

Then you limped back to your car with an empty wallet
with a frown of dried tears.
A fake phone number folded in your pocket.

You were drenched in the darkest of dark,
and I was in my element,
watching and waiting in my car for my share
of the money we earned.

DANCING IN LOS ANGELES

We are just friends set together temporarily.
Take what you can from me and I will exploit the benefits in you.
When we are both fulfilled we can leave with no explanations,
moving from host to host, connecting and swiftly unplugging that
emotional cord that brought us together.

LEECH

Got me paranoid,
don't trust them.
Sometimes they remind me of leeches,
smiling to deceive,
to attach on to your vulnerabilities,
and when they're full they move to the next
host, leaving them weak.
They take his goods while he is shaking on the ground,
crying for life.
And they politely shake their clothes
and walk away wondering why he's still on the ground,
because all they see is weakness or strength.
Although their smiles seem at peace,
beware of the beast that's hungry underneath.

Leech.

EVERYBODY IS A SLAVE

Everybody is a slave.
Why, you're asking me?
Because every creature has a belly.
What is a belly, you're asking me?
Something that feeds the body.
And what is a body?
Something fragile that grows old that depends on food to sustain.
Then why are we all slaves, you ask me?
Well, just as cute birds go chirping around our plates
as you smile with delight,
they are chirping because they need food,
not because they want to entertain.
So you're asking me again,
why is every creature a slave?
Well, the birds wake up in the morning to feed their babies,
as the wolves that have no choice but to hunt the buffalo,
just as all creatures that hide from the sun to desperately steal at night from
our trash cans.
And we are all slaves when we wake up early to clock into our jobs,
to greet strangers and speak things not from the heart with a plastic grin,
never sincere, like there was some type of mask plastered on our face that
could never fit.
"Hello, sir, how are you?"
"Hello, ma'am, so happy to see you!"
And we say we want to be free,
always forgetting that we were all born with this burden.
And we can lie to ourselves to say we are fine all alone,
but while we have this thing
we will get in line,
we will do what we can.

THE BASICS AGAIN

Over the years I evolved tough as the skin of a wolverine.
The wolves bite like always, but it is only like a pinch.
I fight back, then they run away again with snarling teeth.
Just another day to fight, eat, and rest.
There is nothing so beautiful and new for my eyes to see.

Then if so, God, show me?

He looks up at the sky, receiving no answer.

A woman walks by. He then glances at the woman. "Can someone please show me?"

The woman ignores him.

He smiles.

Like I was saying . . . life is mundane.

And I am too intelligent.

I live in a zoo.

RAT SPOKE TO THE STARLIT SKY

If I am nothing, then why are you trying to teach me?
I am just here wandering and looking at all these things my eyes can't understand.
And you say I am nothing but my pain feels real.
So nothing is painful?
And now nothing is something?
How do you want me to be thankful if I am a separate nothing?
First of all, I can only experience myself.
Second, I am nothing but I can feel and speak, and I am lonely so my words are full of sorrow.
How else would you expect a lonely nothing to speak?
With ease? Ha!
If you are nothing then don't speak, don't allow me to see.
Don't bring this light to matter making me a me.

You great master . . .

MAGNOLIA FLOWER

The warmth of her full lips caught me by surprise.
I watched her brown skin, which reminded me of the earth made into a woman.

And her heart— made of a gently woven bird's nest— bringing me home.
And her lips— a blooming magnolia flower coming into full bloom

into my own lips— taking me away from the cold.

BROKEN ONE

Broken spirits cry while the earth screams.
How did it get this way?
I get cold,
distant,
but I want to kiss you.
But from a distance,
because I know at this time,
this time,
when the world screams,
you scream and I sometimes scream.
But the only peace I found is within me,
so forgive me if I can't touch you,
hug you,
be near you,
because through my experiences you have taught me.

Yes, you have taught me.

STARING AT THE RAIN

Just want to be washed in it,
let it come through my body
and merge into me and we become one.
I don't care—
Take it all,
all my pain.
On rainy days like this, I always waited for this moment.
On lonely nights where I contemplated on why, if I love this deep, where is
my wife?
Too much passion wasted, like one hundred dollar bills thrown out of car
windows.
God, show me how to use it.
I want to be there in it, not just on the sideline watching.
Thinking of my life as just limits to me is pointless.
God, take me there.
I want to go there, regardless of the consequences.

LET IT RAIN

I am okay
with the burning in my heart,
like coals burning slow.
What an indescribable pain
of the poet and artist,
and the masks that we wear
to not be exposed,
of the beauty that is kept inside.
How joyful is life,
to know that even pain happily passes by.
And in the shadows,
there is a love and a warm embrace
that cannot be seen with the human eye
at the end of the ride.
Goodbye,
goodbye,
goodbye.
So let the rain trickle down these feet of mine.
I embrace life, and I am no longer afraid to die.

JUNKIE AT A BAR

I like unhealthy things.
Nasty women,
fried foods,
sweet things with no nutrition.
God created taste buds, but we can't taste?
I want to taste because it feels so good.
You are probably the same.
Yeah, you lie a lot.
I bet you never had sex;
I bet you never liked the feeling of being drunk.
You are great.

GOD LIKE THE GRAY SKY

I can't change my darkness because that is a part of who I am.
When you walk one step forward while leaving the other step behind,
you are walking toward the light while keeping one foot in the dark.
And to keep this dream going is to keep walking,
keep moving,
keep struggling forward.
Without a struggle, you and I will be a nothing again.

DARKNESS SPEAKS

You always deny me,
but every creature comes out of me.
Even I'm a part of your mother, the Earth you call her.
I was there when you came out of the womb, and I took you to the light you
desired.
And when you got older and sick, I would comfort you and take you back
home when the sun could do nothing but shine light over your wounds.
I come because I care, not because I have to.
I am also loving, like the light you desperately seek,
and I really do love you, but you have to understand,
with all my work with every creature and every plant on this Earth,
I never get any credit for my love.
And you only call me when you have no more options,
but I understand.

You don't understand my purpose.
But because I don't live as dense as you, I will always remember why I am
here.

LIGHT SPEAKS

I am the light you all seek.
I am what you call love,
but I am not what you imagined love to be.
A spark of me reminds you of what's inside.
As I see, you have met darkness, who also loves as pure as I.
And I don't hate her, because she is my sister.
She brings you here and then takes you home,
but I keep you here until you leave, then I stay here,
waiting until you see me in the skies again.
My small little creatures, I love you, just like you imagined.
When you reach out in the air to touch my hand,
I will always be on your side.
I am on every beautiful face you desired,
and inside the uglies of the world you constantly left behind.
What I'm trying to teach you, my dear children, is the deeper light,
the light that I really am.

When you become bitterly ungrateful,
striking against all that you see from selfish eyes,
and striking against your own roots that keep you standing,
that is when my sister comes to whisper in your ears,
blinding your eyes from behind.

CUT HER OFF

I dive in oceans,

jump off of skyscrapers
to detach her,

to dodge that familiar sting
when I think,

when I see

others that resemble her.

I delete her number for the last time,

go jogging in the woods
while beating my chest.

Got to scream when I'm running.
Got to really pull these hooks someway, somehow.

Got to really throw them,
then I'm free out of this hell.

Call me crazy,
but you look sober and insane.

I ran when my momma was beating my ass
as a little boy,

and you stayed.

A FEARFUL MAN

Cut her off before she becomes complacent and cold.
Seen it all so many times before.
A smart man was a man who left without turning back.

On to the next train
On to the next

And they like my force
My coldness
My detachment

They seem puzzled to know that I know their game better than what they
had planned all along.

DARK MAN

I seen an older man who reminded me of myself,
dark-skinned and all,
drunk on the Los Angeles streets.
When he spoke, I laughed.
We both laughed because we could relate to the bitter cold.
We knew each other very well.
He said "Hi" to every person that walked by,
and they never replied,
and we both laughed so hard again.

Near Union Station 2014

BOUNDARIES

I tried to knock on your door
to try and break the boundaries you speak,
but you greeted me with a distant smile
and closed the door on my feet.
I didn't want to go to war,
I didn't want you to apologize.
I just wanted to get an understanding,
look you in your eyes
to see what you see.
And I wanted you to see where I've been,
but you treated me like you didn't see me.
Do I make you uncomfortable when I speak?
I want you to come out of the closet and stop being so scared.
I want to come out of the closet and not be so scared about this topic.

Why can't we be free and speak?
Our differences are what we are,
our similarities are what we are.
Seems like we haven't gotten too far,
but they say we are free.
Are we?

Come on, why can't we really be free?

NO CHOICES

You didn't ask to be white.
I didn't ask to be black.
Nature does not care.
It creates, then turns a blind eye.

WE ALWAYS WANT MORE

The grass always seems greener on the other side when you are with some-one over a long period of time, with only a few problems and few dislikes.

And what is over the large pearly gates so far away will always seem better than what you already have.

But I say keep her; there is nothing greater on the other side.
And I say continue to love him, because there will always be dull moments of time.

To the both of you, there will always be a lack of mystery.
The magic between both of your hearts will come in moments of surprises.

And the lack of spark in your hearts will many times linger, and the absence of lust and the absence of pleasure will also continue from moment to moment.

But those are the seasons, like the hidden pathways leading to the gates of future beautiful moments.

To you, my lovely sister,
and to you, my lovely brother,
we have become too shortsighted to see the whole picture.

A relationship is a garden that constantly needs plowing and watering.

Striving through hard times together are the seeds planted for the next beautiful seasons to come.

WHEN THE FIRE SPOKE

I let go of it all.
I don't want anything anymore!
I don't know what your plans are for me, God, but I let go!
I just let go!
All the things that I desired I don't care about anymore.
I am just going to let go and I'm not going to expect anything.
My life will be full of things I can't understand.
I understand that now, because I give up on trying so hard to catch the wind.
You have to understand, I tried so hard to go against the grain.
I traveled up the hill barefoot, covered in sweat and blood from my back to my toes.
I kicked the wall drunk, I broke everything that was around me, I lost my mind.
I cried alone, and I didn't want anyone to hold me, and I didn't want to apologize.
And honestly I still don't understand what I felt, but I know it was real.
I won't lie to you or anybody anymore,
I won't pretend—
I won't calm down the fire that is burning inside of me.
I won't act like I am too proud, when inside I feel like a hungry wolf cornered, but all I know is war.
God, help me become peace.
Help me learn to trust, and help me love again.
Because I am fire, and I pray that you will one day bless me with rain.

My heavenly Father,
I just want to be free.

NOTHING REMAINS

I see the most beautiful mountains fall.
The most beautiful song that passed me by.
The kiss I wanted to cherish has gone.

I can only be that change that life is.
Things rise and fall, as life and death.

My strength is in change because life as I know is change.

Although I dwell in pain, I smile in the midst of war.

Let pain rinse off my back like rain washing off a sword covered in blood
into the pearly gates.

I cannot hold on to nothing here.
I cannot own anything here.
I cannot even make love, not even on the stars, because tomorrow I may be
in the grave.

TRUTH IS

Truth is just a breath.

People tell me to believe, but I don't believe in anything.
I know nothing because I am nothing.
And everything I feel will fade, being that human civilization is just a second amongst the universe.

So what do I believe?

I just observe,
listen,
sip tea,
sometimes box assholes if they corner me.

I'm sorry I'm not that easy.
You can label me as a religious man, maybe just a humble
man, but find me on the street cursing because shit hurts when you fall
head-on.

I admit things that sometimes we all will not admit.
Like I'm biased because I'm a man.
I am biased because I can't see the whole picture from my narrow eyes, just
like most of you.

And I'm still working on it, but I know this is just an illusion. I hate hiding.

You want my truth? Keep asking.

I love you even if I don't like you.
I heard this doesn't matter.
I heard love is the only real thing.

What I believe? I don't know.

I just observe,
listen,
sip tea,
sometimes box assholes if they corner me.

COUNTRY ME

I was just a little boy walking barefoot
in Tennessee near the woods
behind a tree with my BB gun.
Ten years old, swimming in a pond with no shoes,
saving up money to buy some candy.
Wondering what if I could meet some pretty girls
when I get my new church shoes.
I remember fishing with my father.
Hunting without shooting nothing.
I remember how I wondered about God.

Didn't think about race.
Didn't think about poverty.
Until the world told me
what to do.

BROTHER HERBIE

It was always humility with him.
The crowd laughed and mocked him in a small church in Henderson,
Tennessee.
And I remember before church started, I once saw him behind the church
building taking a small bottle out of his suit jacket.
He had one bigger foot than the other,
so he walked with a limp,
licking his own wounds in the dark with alcohol on his breath.
He stood in front of the church singing the same song with great passion,
and they still laughed at him.
But now I got older; I realize how beautiful he was.

I'M NOT A MAN

I made all of this up in my head.
I was trapped between her legs.
I know, I'm supposed to be stronger, but for once let me tell you my deepest
dreams.
Like I said, her legs surrounded me, trapped me.
Her lips fixed to mine, and her arms tight around me with no space in
between.
My head pressed to her breast,
then her lips pecking on top of my head gently, intently.
I know, I know, I'm supposed to be the strong one here,
but let me tell you, it was my deepest dreams.
She rocked me to sleep. She had the embrace I wasn't used to.
But she was beautiful, rocking me into tears.

Slowly kissing my wounds . . .

IT IS NOT TRUE

Women should know more about a man's body.
It is not a piece of steel.
Not a piece of hardware they can cheaply buy.
Not a hard table to slam their heels on.
Our hands are not made of brick.
Our skin was made to be kissed.
Our heads were made to be caressed.
You, as a woman, should throw away the books titled *What Men Like*, written by rich women detached from reality.
You should throw away the wisdom about men from your auntie, grandma, and girlfriends.

ABOUT WOMEN

Let me speak of women:

supple like flowers on a field under a somber sky,

and those are the flowers drooping lowly,
hiding until the sun's rays come shining in.

Let me go on:

Sometimes she smiles like a large, bright sun rising in the morning,
but that smile never remains.

And then she has the eyes of the night sky,
locking into the depths of the unknown;
her eyes swiftly become detached from my eyes,

catlike . . .

And what I always feared was her unknown strength,
her ability to adjust,
her patience,
her silence.

Then she surprises me, stepping closer to me, speaking about her vulner-
abilities, sounding soft and open.
And I am puzzled by her sudden change, and I am subtly and slowly tender-
ized by her presence.
Hearing her words like soft cotton, noticing her shapely porcelain legs
relaxed near my body, her essence pulling me in closer, like the speechless
words to describe waves moving.

Tranquil, as if I was reading a book in the grass,
and there she came, with some strange ways,
beautiful and inviting. Asking me, "Can we whisper things about life together?"

Just when I wanted to throw anything about women away.

I marched home privately angry.
Just as I love the openness, it always hurts the most sooner or later.

But like I was saying,

let me speak of the women I have always known:

elusive as attempting to catch rain with my bare hands.
Even if I caught her, she would eventually turn into vapors.

Moving,
whispering things
sounding like music,
penetrating through my body and moving past me
to an endless field of sunshine where new men with their new mysteries and
their new possibilities are.

It was always up and down,
the sun would fall,
and they would fall limp, appearing fragile,
and rise gracefully and confidently as soon as the sun rose back up again.

STRENGTH OF BUTTERFLIES

Let me speak of women

Flowers, sunsets, and the night sky

Let me speak of women

Pulling me in like rain,
a cold stare, thick walls

Let me go on about women

Not enough in the world's eyes
and many times misunderstood

Let me tell you what I know about women

Beautiful
unpredictable
flexible

Immortal

THE BLACK BOY ON THE BUS

I'm protected by my imagination.
You can't bring me down
although you are choking me to sleep.
I am shedding tears underneath, but I am smiling
because my mind stays under the pier
where the dark waves flow,
where no other man dares to dwell.

He pauses.

No matter what you do or say,
I will have my way, and you will have yours.
He imagined the world's eyes indifferent, boxed off, and judgmental.

He shook his head.

I told you I am not going to throw away my confidence.
I am smart without your validation.
I will not put my head down to make any of you comfortable.
I will be like a strength you have no choice but to adhere to.

He begins to smile.

I will teach you to only come to me as a man,
looking at me without false smiles or guilt.
Then I will greet you equally.

SHE KISSED A DYING OAK TREE

She slowly grew on him, surrounding his body with brown mold and green moss.

He can't escape her detachment, her selfless embrace.
Her love is only needed from one time to another,
like one plant from another, growing and then dying.

And what was that he hoped for but could never find while he was alive?

Some type of love with attachment?
She broke him moistly and slowly, piece by piece, while his body sunk deeper into her wet body as the sun and rain touched him.

Right before he died he heard the voice of her, "Shhh, my child, who thinks so highly of himself."

"You come into me, and I will use you as you are needed!
Broken, back into my body, back under my streams of water,
back into the cold, soft soil, back where you were born.

You will be used as food for my small creatures.
You will be used to fertilize the gardens of my skin.

The tulips in autumn, the dandelions in spring, they all wait to rise and see the rays of the sun just as you did."

LOVERS' RUBIK'S CUBE

A bitter drunk
is a dreamer

A prostitute
is a giver

A suicidal man
thinks too much

A happy man
is just a simple man

Because a happy man
married Barbara

A miserable man
tried to marry Barbie

I go home single, simple and
drunk.

A poor, lonely poet
wrote about beautiful women.

And a rich man
paid to keep them,
and all the women preferred him over the poorer ones.

But they said he was too cold because he thought they only wanted what he
had, not who he truly was.

Poor men, rich or broke,
you will never gain what you truly desire.

You will try, but it will be as comforting as tightly embracing a stem of thorns in your hands, and then pressing it against your lips.

You will try to keep it there, to say you truly do believe in love, but it will be so painful, eventually it will give you no other choice but to let go.

UNDER OUR FEET

Life is pain:
I want to dress it up.
Sweeten it up.
Polish it.
Romanticize it.
But it will always find its way:
bare, rooted, and weeping amongst itself.

The world is too large for me to try to embellish it.
It hates my shallow idea of beauty and my idea of comfort.

It will go on with its children: birthing and dying,
attending only to their basic needs as it always did.

The babies cry from the womb— the new light shining on their winced
eyes.
And the bones under the deep soil rot and deteriorate from what used to
be bitter pleas and unanswered prayers.

A HOMELESS MAN FINDS LOVE

In the wilderness

I imagined food to eat because I didn't have any.

In the wilderness

I would carve wood into flutes to play so I could sing with the birds.

In the wilderness

I forgot how it feels to be touched by another human.

In the wilderness

I learned to walk among pain because I learned how to heal from plants and roots.

In the wilderness

I prayed to God for a woman that was for me and sometimes I just gave up, but I will never give up.

He took a small bottle out of his jacket, and then took a quick swig.
He then looked around his surroundings with a small spark in his eyes of drunken brilliance.

"I look around this place . . .

This beautiful place . . .

To see she is all around . . . "

The city bus loudly moved by as a plastic bag flew from the street, gliding to the ground near him. And cars beeped their horns against each other as they waited at a stoplight a block ahead.

He was sitting next to a water fountain that had no water.
It had a dirty newspaper and dirtied napkins laying in it.

VULNERABLE AGAIN

Being vulnerable again—
Uh oh, I look at myself and I know that I am spirit in the flesh.
I can't deny that I want your touch.
It would be like saying that I was meant to die alone,
and this makes me vulnerable again.
But I guess I am up for the ride,
the strong tides,
and days where I wonder how to handle all of this openness again.
Vulnerable again,
here I go again
I think I have no choice but to go on this ride.

MAN IN A CAGE

I've been listening to their conversations.
Got me quietly observing,
and it occurred to me
that they all say the same thing,
one after another.
Got me in the mirror checking myself,
touching my face,
feeling insane.
Ladies talk and talk like the clicking of the clock on
the wall, from my sister to the lady across the way,
repeating the same experience again and again,
and honestly I hate this game.
And I guess that's just human nature;
survival of the fittest helps the weak become strong.
Whatever happened to the good old knight?
The man of heart?
And the woman who loved the man who crawled before he walked?
I'm angry, with conflicting thoughts.
Trying not to sound like the victim,
so I keep it to myself,
but instead of staying the prey I become the predator.
If not the predator, let me put on my shield
to protect these delicate emotions of mine.
Got my game face sharp like rugged edges of a steel sword,
and they ask me, "What is wrong?"
Inside I'm like, "What do you mean, what's wrong?
Nothing's wrong!"
Veins coming out of my face,
thoughts racing the race.
This fire inside of me burning hot.

Looking in the mirror again,
I change my thoughts
and my emotions change.
I'm paranoid,
can't trust anyone, and I am
distant, going for the distance,
to money, loneliness, and fame,
forever no one to blame.
My anger remains.

Sweating vodka from my face,
my heart forever protected
behind a rusty steel cage.

THE DRUNK MAN WHO KNEW

A woman wants to love.
A woman wants to nurture.
I'm so sorry, baby,
you just don't love them when they good.
You understand.
I understand.
I know you, woman.
Even if you don't want to be with him,
you want to love him.

CAREFUL

Why do I think about you?
Don't want you, but when I think of you a feeling hits my chest.
Honestly I don't like it;
sometimes I do.
Sometimes I think of you and smile.
Sometimes I wish you can understand why I don't talk to you anymore.
I'm just scared of being hurt, just like any other man.
I hope I can get over this feeling.
I hope you know that I take hits hard because I love hard.
Baby, I got to work.
Baby, I got to keep smiling.

HER BODY

Something is deep about a woman's body.

I'm not talking about having sex.

Something I've been afraid to say, people have been afraid to say.

It is as beautiful as her lips and all of her other godly parts.

I am in love with it, and I don't know why.

I guess I never understand why everybody wants to travel so far to stare at the ocean.

That is how a woman's body is for me. I wish I could understand, and I don't. I am just a fool looking, dazed like we all look at the ocean, just looking, wondering.

No wonder a man can be a fool, just see the way we look when she comes walking.

Here comes a living ocean:

moving,

flowing.

We not knowing how much depth or power she has

while we glance at her hips as she walks,

and the power exuding from her arms

going down to her soft and full hands.

We crave those hands . . .

And we crave something from her that cannot be put into words.

It's subtle, but so powerful.

Even if I could convey it in words, I doubt she would understand.

If I told her all that I feel, I would be too vulnerable.

She would know I secretly worship her.

I want her near, just as I want the ocean near.
I want to put my feet in the cool waters
and allow the small waves to gently touch them.
Just as I want my body with her hands
along with her tilted head
from one moment to another, touching.

FISHING

I watch her from a distance staring into space,
and then shifting her eyes my way.
I feel her eyes on my hand, while my hand touches my tilted head.
I pretend I see nothing, like a possum in the dark.
I know nothing of her eyes,
I say to myself with a smile within my mind.
Now the second time she goes glancing again.
Then the third time, and now I know— she bit the bait.
I could reel it in, but—
I would throw it back home after I see her too weak and afraid.
My weakness is that I am too strong.
It is like a bear trying to tickle a turtle that hides in its shell.
I asked God to take me where the giants are.

I wouldn't have to put my head down,
soften my voice,
hide my muscles anymore.

I'M A MAN, TOO

He is bitterness and too much cologne.
A man masked in disguise.

I despise his smell
I hate his jealousy
I hate his lies of manhood

His stories of the military are always embellished.
He speaks of football loudly to please his brothers.
I do not believe him.
I always stay far away from him.

And there he goes for the first attack.

He rattles the crowd to get attention first, like always.
He is like a bull with no brain, rushing to a sword hidden behind my back.

And there he is, on the ground
The crowd-their mouths open
And there he is, still laying on the ground
The sound of the ambulance is coming

And I look at him on the ground, just like I always look at men who believed
that real manhood can only be displayed by being the loudest and the most
aggressive.

He was foolish to believe I am not a man as well.

THE COMING OF WINTER

Dear Sunshine,

I have the window open to see you.
I haven't contemplated you for a while,
and before you go, I am now reminded to be thankful of your infinite love.

And now I see the winds moving the leaves.
This means, she will soon come . . .

And before I can hear her transparent, cold body moving against the front door, and then her footsteps of small, grey bodies with their many small, beady eyes quietly screeching on the wood floor and drifting into dark corners,

I must say, I am sorry. I didn't appreciate you like I do now.

But I suppose, there's more to winter than crisp, cold wind.

The flame on a lit candle that I placed near the window now sways briskly like always when she comes.

Her husky, feminine voice now speaks, rattling against the window I have just closed.
The sound of invisible feet moves again as it pleases.
My room again colder and colder.

And I will soon hide myself in covers,
hearing her concerns about me,
then her body feeling like icy wind near mine until the sun rises.

BLACK PEOPLE

The warmth of black people
is sweeter than you would believe.
We are not perfect, just as any other
race, but we have our ways.
We are unique people.

WALKING IN SADNESS TO AUTUMN

It pulls my chest
and sinks my head.
It dulls my mind
and aches my hands.
It drains my voice
but erases my fears.
The leaves fall, brown
and slowly, step by

        step,

a crackling under my feet.

My runny nose
and my numb face
against the forceful cold
accompanied by a silver flask in my stiff hand.
And still, not a smile surfaced on my face,
but there is magic
all around.

And the sullen breaths among the desolate trees,
colliding at my jacket.
And the smell of a new beginning in the air
that reminds me of her
brisk
cold
fingers
softly touching my arm.

HIS BEST FRIEND AND WHISKEY

It was her, then her, then another,
who all spoke of love so passionately
and nothing lasted but his dog who licked his heart.
Then there were nights where he drank whiskey and he had unknowingly
opened the gates of heaven, and he felt an ocean of stars moving above.
And in this, he smiled a real smile.
A realistic happiness, he thought to himself,
as his dog steadily watched his movements to show him more affection as he
gazed at the large tires of his truck parked outside of his window while the
sun, large and orange, slowly sank down.

GATES TO HEAVEN

I work a full-time job.
I have a small, warm place to live with no kitchen.
A cabinet full of exotic teas and a drawer with an old typewriter and
unopened whiskey bottles on top.
I have just enough food to get by, but I see something I didn't see before.
I'm becoming more thankful, although . . .

Well, let me go on to tell you.

I was in pain my whole life because my problem was that I was too deep,
and the world isn't so deep. It is functional, practical; it is business-oriented.

So this brings me to two essential questions:

How much should a poem cost?
What is the urgency of a poem to the world?

To my fellow poets

I promised myself, this year, not to be so deep.
And if so, let it fade away in my closet until I am a successful poet.

A word to my fellow poet:
The world does not take you seriously.

But regardless, write when you get off of work.
Write when you imagine a love you do not have.
Write when that knife strikes the heart again and again,

because we have no wings to fly from this place.
So let our pens be our saviors.
Let our poems and short stories and novels be the consistency we all search
for.
And if you have true friends and family who love you, you are already rich
even if you are not famous.
And if you become famous, remain with those who love you;
then I will tell you, you already have the keys to heaven.

A practical heaven.

It is that simple

The world does not need another yoga mat.
The world does not need another hero.
The world does not need another prayer alone in a room where no one can
hear the cries of the heart but yourself.

The world needs honesty.
The world needs their stomachs full.
The world needs more drinks among laughter and conversation.

Drunks chattering until the sun rises,

then do it again next week,
and again the other,
until every drop is drunk,
and every word from the heart is spoken.

TREES

A forest
of trees leaning in different directions—
intertwining their legs,
their arms,
their brown necks stretched.

They trapped me,
comforted me,
gave me fruit when I was hungry.
I patiently stayed there, satisfied
with the burning in my heart,

watching their hands of leaves,
their extended boughs.

I was fed full many times,
and I didn't care what they whispered
or what they would do if I stayed.

I was there
even when it drizzled and when it rained.

I stayed there
with no worries.

I watched them steadily and silently moving as if they were not moving at
all, and it appeared there was no time in that space.

Every movement and every touch amplified love—
The morning dew on their arms,
the smell of honeysuckle,
flowery perfumes spilled in the air,
and how could I forget?

The soft caress of wind
moving against my flesh.

How can I get the thought of being there out of my mind?

How can I ever forget?
In the middle of their arms,
their legs,
their stretched bodies wrapped around me.
There, where love trapped me.

1994

HOPES OF SUNSHINE

My hidden smile saw her finger caress his palm tenderly,
but only in my mind.

His heart fluttered,
so beautiful it was embarrassing,
but only in my mind.

These types of moments in my head are precious as pearls hidden away in
the depths of darkness, like my thoughts kept behind a large wall.

But I smiled secretly that day, watching intently her fingers in the palm of
his hand.
It was as if the sun was shining in the color gray.
If only I could somehow pause that moment, as if it could last forever,
but only in my mind.

HEART OF SEASONS

The heart changes its song every season.
The heart beats and flutters differently every season.

Can you smell it coming?

Can we continue to hold hands in this season?

But I would love for us to walk in many seasons to come.

And if there is heartache, my Lord, we will shelter ourselves by giving each other a little distance. Or we can protect our hearts with no words further spoken, by only caressing our hearts with our hands until deep sleep.

Oh my Lord, my heart beats too strong in winter.

Then it sings softly in spring.

In summer, it waits in shades, not knowing what will come.

WORRY ALONE

When you are at the cafe alone…and the season is changing…
you can feel everything in your stomach-life changes.
The people you love, whom you secretly worry about.
And you don't know what will happen next to you. What is life?

A struggle and change of seasons all at once, it seems.

IT CONTROLS US

This morning I did a terrible thing.
My heart burned slow as if someone lit it on fire.
I didn't know what to do—
I prayed for it to go away
and paced while I felt its pain.

Am I like all animals in this world,
controlled by that thing that makes male birds
sing until the sun goes down,

that thing that makes a ram slam his head into
another male's head, to gain her respect?

I hate this, God have mercy on me.

But I am sure my cry, Lord, will be ignored
or laughed at, because even as a human being,
I am not exempted from nature's cruelty of the heart.

I have no protection . . .

My attempt to find love is the same as any other
small creature in the forest in search for love.

TO THE BUTTERFLY

If only my soul was light as a butterfly, I would feel purity in life again.

Today, a woman kissed my cheek, and I was happily awakened with a little more relief than I had years before her kiss. But I know, she, like a butterfly, must leave and fly freely to one flower to another.

I'm afraid my inner urge for attachment to what cannot be keeps my muscles aching and my mind numbing cold, as if I sleep with my head submerged in ice.

I must work until I can no longer feel anymore and moan freely behind closed doors to know I tried everything I could to adapt to the freedom of our modern world. "Love must be free," they say. The butterfly sings and loves that song as if God wrote it for her. I do not understand that song.

And my heart is never light—I live in heavy solitude, yearning for a lover who will take me till death. And I do not seek freedom or to dance under the rays of the sun.

The strength of my arms' embrace is similar to the strength you see in the distant, ice-capped mountains.

And my kiss is with meaning, almost painful, as if it is the hopeful and tender bite of a wolf to another wolf, but when it is done, you know it is from a man who truly loves.

And my spirit is not carefree. If it is so, it is only for a short moment, like a moth's wings flickering drunkenly across the door lights into death.

SEA AT NIGHT

The trials of our days will have little relief,
and our hearts are neglected and muddied.
I dream of a place, of an embrace, that is tender and true
because the mask we wear is uncomfortable, heavy, tight, and uneven.

If I could choose where I go in my dreams, then I would feel some sense of freedom.

Imagine lying amongst large black boulders when you open your eyes. The sea is black and strong against that shore you lie on, and the sky is illuminated by bright stars above.

Then to hear the words of a woman you know so well.

And those words would tell you to close your eyes. "Life is a dream and this is your place of refuge."

You would be free, and the sound of those waves would be a joyous memory during your awakening day.

LITTLE BY LITTLE

In winter, the heart feels like
pieces of thin, broken glass are scattered within it.
Where does this emotion come from?
Why is the face stuffy and numb?

You tuck in what may hurt you more
as a turtle would hide in its shell when a storm comes.

There are times when doing little is good

and being consistent will get you out of the agony to a temporary peace.

Crippled you maybe, but you find your own way,

limping slowly from one bottle to the other. If that is what you have to do to
smile once in a while, then so be it.

A WINTER DAY

I clock out of my job,
Walk home with the cold air of winter,
And I'm just a small mouse amongst
a bigger world in the city of Los Angeles.

My runny nose—but this season I humbly accept the changes around me
and in me.
The wind piercing my chest—
Silver and gold horns play a slow festive tune from men in snug coat jackets,
And a red metal can in front of them rattles for change.

The loneliness of men, some sitting on the sidewalk,
some at coffee shops wearing the same clothes they wore yesterday.

And I enter my cluttered room,
Taking off my suit,
The whiskey bottle awaits.

I want nothing now, because sober, my love is irrelevant.

I SMILED AGAIN

I felt a victory in something I can't put into words tonight.
It was something that could not be bought.
I was rich, and I remain so, without owning much of anything.
And walking these streets with words of books in my mind,
with the sweet wind gently to my face.

And it's okay.

Tonight I live . . .

And tonight I finally smile once again!!!
And maybe in days to come, I will live again the way I live now.

LION

I

Not one embrace of another's hand can help me grow wings.
Not one other heart can light my own heart on fire, unless
I become the Lion I am.

II

A Lion that runs past
those who wait politely in line.

III

I must learn to fight again,
not live life hiding from death.

GOD AND THE POOR

We live in the trenches
humbly knowing
nothing is guaranteed.
But somehow, there is beauty
walking lowly.
Warmth is accepting
the changes of life naturally as death,
and the unpredictable circumstances it brings us.
Warmth does not pretend.
It does not lie.
The poor are richer
because we show our tears.
That is warmth,
closer to God.
We do not pretend we
are incapable of suffering.
We sing the blues.

The rich pay to learn sadness.

Poems edited by Wonoh Massaquoi
Front cover photography by BeeJavier

ABOUT HEAVY THINGS

J.G. Finch wrote *Heavy Things* while living in a small, closet-sized room in an old hotel in Pasadena. Most poems were written from J.G. Finch's real experiences and from him wandering the streets at night, taking it all in. In *Heavy Things*, Finch paints his emotions into words. From the eyes of a simple, poor black man living in America, Finch captures the subtle emotions of an average man who struggles with alcohol abuse, lack of money, and heartache. In several poems, Finch jostles with racism and writes about the idea of suicide and the limitations of love. He then surprisingly writes in an arrogantly confident way, as if waiting on the right moment to yell checkmate, before winning the game against an uninformed player:

"He is bitterness and too much cologne.
A man masked in disguise.

I despise his smell
I hate his jealousy
I hate his lies of manhood

His stories of the military are always embellished.
He speaks of football loudly to please his brothers.
I do not believe him.
I always stay far away from him.

And there he goes for the first attack.

He rattles the crowd to get attention first, like always.
He is like a bull with no brain, rushing to a sword hidden behind my back.

And there he is, on the ground
The crowd-their mouths open
And there he is, still laying on the ground
The sound of the ambulance is coming"

Poems from *Heavy Things* are a well-crafted mix of beautiful subtleties with a surprising strength of muscle, and words that are deep, honest, and melancholy. The span of different emotions in *Heavy Things,* gives this work a more interesting balance than many other poetry books.

Finch's writing does not follow the stereotypes of most disadvantaged artists. His writing is his alone and is not from the influence of others telling him how he is supposed to write.

First and foremost, I would like to thank God.

And thank you to all the people who believed in me.

*To all my **fans**, let's stay in touch...*

www.jgfinch.com